Justin Tso

Navajo Painter of Legends

By

Virginia Benderly

© 2002, Wind Song Publisher
P.O. Box 608, Patagonia, AZ   85624
ISBN 0-9718159-0-9

This book is dedicated to the spirits of those who went before,
whose voices may be heard on the canyon winds;
and to Alice, whose great rug graces my home.

Acknowledgments

No book is ever written without the help of others. I gratefully acknowledge those who have helped me. First, the subject of this book, Justin Tso, who with his wife Evelyn, spent hours driving back and forth from Canyon de Chelly to Patagonia and talking into a tape recorder, to tell me the stories of his childhood and the beliefs of his people.

Eddie Draper, who helped so much with the physical properties of taking apart frames so the photographs could be made without the glare of glass.

Rod Brown, my long suffering and very patient editor who has helped me with my last two books, and who continues to be my friend in spite of it. I'm sure he thinks I will never learn how to put a book together without the use of commas in almost every sentence.

Bill Haas, whose expertise in photography made the paintings come to life.

And of course, my husband, Shaw, who read and re-read the manuscript, corrected my grammar and didn't complain of the hours I had to spend sitting at my computer. My thanks to you all.

All paintings in this book are from the collection of the author.

Introduction

Canyon de Chelly is in the north-east corner of Arizona. It is a place of mystery, a place of drama, a riot of color. When one listens, the winds speak in hushed voices; when it is stormy, the voices grow loud and angry. The floor of the canyon can be a bed of water, or in the dry season, a bed of sand. In the winter snow fills the hollows and makes the canyon a place to be admired from the rim.

Those who have been privileged to visit the area come away with a sense of awe, knowing they have seen a miracle of nature. But those few who have known the canyon from their birth are among the most blessed of men.

Such a person is the subject of this book. Justin Tso. Born in the canyon, raised in and near the canyon, drawing his spiritual nourishment from the canyon, he has allowed his paintings to illustrate not only the landscape with which he is so familiar, but the many symbols that tell the stories, the legends, the deep beliefs of his people, the Diné, the Navajo.

Her Loom Is Silent

Her loom is silent now.

Only the soft wind remembers her songs

as her fingers wove the colored yarns,

creating the pattern held in her mind.

Her hands are quiet now.

Only the heart remembers the soothing touch

when night ghosts walked, and fears

clutched the heart of a small child.

Her voice is silent now.

Only the soul remembers her whispers

to the spirits of her people, the Holy Ones,

blessing her family with their protection.

The pot that held the mutton stew is empty now.

Only the strong bodies of her children

remember the food that was more than food.

Her loom is silent now.

Her heart is quiet now.

She lives in the beauty she created.

The Early Years

It was a cold November in 1946, and the Tso family was preparing to leave the canyon floor, where they had spent the summer farming and tending their sheep. They would go back to their homes on the rim, where it would be a little warmer and the snows not so deep. The year had been rather dry, and the harvest was late. The family had already stored their corn, and were getting ready to leave for the rough trip to the rim where they would remain for the winter.

The wagons were loaded, and the man, Guy Tso, his wife Alice, who was heavily pregnant, and his children, were ready. Then sudden pains doubled his wife over and he knew she could not make the tough wagon trip up to the rim. There was no choice but to stay where they were, so the baby was born in the canyon. He was called Justin; and in the Navajo way, he was born to Edge Water and born for Coyote Path, the clans of his mother and father.

Justin's great-great-great-grandparents had lived in and around the Canyon before the time when Kit Carson rounded up the Navajos and sent them on the long trek to New Mexico. They had farmed the area, raising corn, squash, watermelons, pumpkins and green beans, and perhaps a small patch of alfalfa. Their hogans were up on the rim of the Canyon, so the sunlight hours would warm their homes during the cold winters, while in the canyon itself, the snow would pile up in the deep shadows.

When spring came they would go back down to their farm areas, where the run-off from melting snow gave ample water to raise their crops. It was a peaceful time. The terrible 'long walk' would come later.

When Justin was a very small boy he would go in and wake his grandfather. They would get up early in the morning to meet the dawn, to speak to the Holy People, to let them know they were ready to start a new day. Justin was taught to meet the dawn. He knew that each morning a Holy Person came with a bag over his shoulder, filled with the good things of life, and if he found the people sleeping he would go on through and they wouldn't get anything.

Even at that young age Justin and horses were almost inseparable. There was one, a roan, that he particularly liked. Some mornings Justin would help saddle the horse, and he and his dad would ride double to the trail head and then to his grandmother's hogan on the rim to get the meat she always had for them. His grandparents had live stock...about 100 head of cattle and two or three hundred head of sheep and goats. When the Tso family needed meat, they would go up that trail and bring back a leg or an arm of goat or sheep, which his grandmother would wrap in a piece of material torn from a flour sack.

When Justin was five his father told him it was now his turn to walk up the trail to his grandmother's hogan and bring back the meat. He and his little dog, Apache, would set out and begin the climb up the trail. His grandmother had sheep dogs that would begin to bark when anyone was coming; then they would go to meet the little boy and walk back to the hogan with him.

Justin loved being there, not only because of the beauty of the area but because he and his grandmother were so close. Always, she would give him a hug and say "Oh, my grandchild is here." He spent as much time as he could with her before taking the meat and starting home. On the way back down the trail the young boy would look for a certain little pine tree. His grandfather had told him the tree was the same age as Justin, and as Justin grew, so did the tree.

As he grew older Justin would help saddle a horse each morning and he and his father would ride double to where his father worked for the National Park Service. Justin would leave his father there and go back to his home. In the afternoon he knew when to catch the roan and saddle him in time to bring his father back. He had cut a heavy branch from a tree and stuck it in the sand. By the way the shadow of the tree fell he could judge the time. He was never late.

While he was still small his father would sing while the boy was taking his bath; perhaps the squaw dance song; or later on toward the winter season, other dance songs. When Justin asked why his father sang, he was told that it was the Navajo way of asking protection for his son. It was unfortunate that his father's influence was lessened so early in his son's life, due to measures beyond anyone's control.

"I have always felt so very close to my grandfather, because he was the one who really raised me in my earliest years. I was told that when I was a small child a deadly sickness came on to the Reservation, and it affected both my parents. They had to be sent off to the Ganado Hospital. I developed some sores on my body and I wasn't growing properly. My grandfather brought a goat into the house and let me drink goat's milk. I really perked up.

"About a week later he had some Navajo policemen drive us over to Ganado to see my mother. My grandfather told me later that I was afraid of her because she had become so thin, just skin and bones and I didn't recognize her. The doctor wanted to fix up my sores but I was afraid to stay there alone, so my grandfather told the doctor that he wouldn't leave me, that he was going to stay with me. The nurse tried to get him out of the room but he said 'no, I am going to stay here with my grandchild.'

"They put me on a bed, washed me and cleaned me up, and sometime in the night I fell out of bed and hit the floor hard! My grandpa got so mad at all those nurses. He said 'people here don't know how to take care of this boy!' He took me out and laid me on a sheepskin and we slept there all night. I guess the sores were just from being undernourished after my mother and father got so sick and had to be taken away. They were in the hospital for over a year, and when they came back I really didn't know they were my mother and dad. My grandpa took their place for those early years, and that's why I have always felt so close to him. He taught me so much - how to greet the dawn, how to run every morning so I would get strong and healthy.

"Sometimes he would tell me to go up to the canyon and bring down the horses. When I got back with them I said, 'What do you want me to do? Where shall I put them?' He would say, 'turn them loose.' I said, 'but I just got them!' 'Turn them loose.' If he had to say it twice, I got the whip! Sometimes at night when it was really cold, I would feel him pulling at my arms to wake me up, and he would take me outside and roll me in the snow. I didn't like that, and I would say 'it's cold, grandpa!' He would say, 'not, it's not. Roll in there!' My mother would tell him he was going to make me sick, but he would always laugh and say 'no, he's going to grow up big and strong.'"

When the family moved back down to the canyon for the summer, Justin's grandfather would take corn pollen and sprinkle it all around the area where they would stay. He asked the canyon to take good care of them, to see that they grew good food. Justin tried to hear the voices that his grandfather could hear, but he never seemed to. When he was herding sheep, he would go up to a big rock and ask it to talk back to him, but he said he never got an answer.

"My brother and a cousin and I were all in the same hogan, and my grandpa's sister was next door. Every morning they would send us to a place called Mule Springs, about a quarter of a mile away. There was a water hole there, pure water, and we kids would go down there to fill the buckets up and bring them back. We'd carry it all the way back home. That's the way we had water.

"Then once a year we'd go hunting. Nowadays, there are poach-ers everywhere all the time. But back then, we would take a deer only once a year, in the traditional way. We were taught not to kill just for the sake of killing. We honored the animals and birds, particu-larly the eagle, because their feathers were our sacred protection.

"I would hear my grandfather singing while he was sitting carv-ing something, and every now and then I would hear a word about a horse. One day I asked him, 'grandpa, can you tell me the name of a male horse and a female horse?'

"He asked why I wanted to know. I said, just because I wanted to know. He said, 'no, because I can look between now and the future and see your life. If you get hold of some of that cheap wine, you'll go talking all over town about how you know the names, and that's not the sacred way of doing it. Not yet, grandchild.'

"All these years he kept it from me. Then one day my wife, Evelyn. and I had a 'good way ceremony', asking that we would be healthy, and our kids would be healthy; even that the horses would be healthy during the tourist season so people could ride in safety. That morning my grandfather decided to come over after everyone else had gone. We were eating breakfast. He came in and sat down and said, 'grandchild ,come here, sit right here beside me.' So I got up and went over to him. He said, 'you wanted to know the name of the horse, didn't you? Now is the time for me to give it to you.' So that year he gave me the name of a mare, a gelding and a stallion. He said, 'never give the name to anyone else. That way you will have many horses.' I made him the promise. He had waited all those years. He knew it was the right time, and that was the year be passed on.

"He was a very wise person. He taught me so many things. He knew that life was going to change, even the land would change, even the sacred places were going to change. And when you see these things, he said, then you will know it is the big change. Nowadays you do see change, people killing relatives, bad things happening. It's really different.

"I was teaching art in the school once, trying to show the kids how things used to be. 'Why is that person dressed like that?' I told him that was the way our grandparents dressed, very colorfully, but they just couldn't understand what I was trying to do - to bring back some of the traditions that are being lost."

Justin's early childhood revolved mostly around his mother and his grandfather. His father, Guy Tso, worked for the National Park Service and was away from home a great part of the time. Only Navajo was spoken at home. One day his grandfather said to him, "Grandchild, one day you are going to school. That man over there, he's going to say, 'Justin, you sweep the floor. You wash your face and brush your teeth. Get a haircut.' That's what he's going to say to you. I want you to think about these things when you go. But there's one thing I don't want you ever to forget - our hogan and your sheepskin. Don't forget those sheep over there, and don't forget your horses."

"The day came when my mother said, 'Justin, you are going to school.' I was a little sad and little apprehensive. I said, 'Mom,

what are they going to do to me? Are they going to whip me? What are they going to do to me over there?'

"She said, 'Justin, I never went to school a day in my life, but you go to school there, and you learn the modern way, things that later on you might use. You might even go to college.'

"The first day in boarding school in Chinle I felt so lonely. They threw towels and sheets at me and said, 'go fix your bed.' I started crying. 'Mom, my grandfather is going to be over there all by himself, he'll have to take care of my sheep. I ought to be with him.'

"My grandma's sister was working for the school and she helped me out a little bit, but I kept asking her, ' When am I going to learn everything so I can go home?'

"The teacher would stand us up and make us stand very straight, and if we didn't, she would give us the ruler. That was in the days when physical discipline was still allowed.

"There were a few kids in the school who were real bullies. They came from town, and used to torment us reservation kids who had herded sheep. I got thrown around a good bit. But what really got to me was the loneliness. This went on for the first month or so. Then we were told we were being allowed to go home for four days for Hallowe'en.

"One by one the kids left with their parents, but no one came for me. There were only one or two of us left, and I started crying. Nobody was coming to get me. I wasn't going home! Then about 5 o'clock I saw my mother walking toward me. I ran to her and hugged her. I didn't want to go back to school, I missed those lambs and goats and my grandfather. We lived only about ten miles from the school but it seemed a long, long way. I stayed in that Chinle school for four years."

Justin's mother was a weaver; her rugs were in great demand from the various trading posts who would commission her to weave rugs for them. His grandfather was a self-taught artist who liked to draw horses.

"When I was, oh, four or five, I used to watch my grandpa. He would cut cardboard boxes real straight with his knife and sit there and draw horses. I used to watch him all the time. He would wet the lead with his mouth and draw. I would say, 'grandpa, that's good. Can I have it?' He would always say, 'no, that's mine. You can't have it.' I have often wished I had some of those drawings, but my mother's big house burned down in 1971 and the pictures were lost. We had a Ceremony then for her, and the medicine man told her the fire was not an accident, that it had been burned on purpose."

Once a month Justin's grandfather would get his pension from the railroad where he had worked in his younger years and he and his grandson would hitch up the wagon and go into the town to the store. One day when Justin was about five, he was watching his grandfather buy the usual canned goods that were kept on shelves or in a big glass case. In that case was a box of watercolor paints. The boy eyed them with longing. He wanted those paints. He wanted to take them and paint a horse. But his grandfather said he couldn't buy them. He told the boy, "go outside and unhitch the horses. Then go over to the feed store

and ask the man for a couple flakes of hay. I've already paid for them, so he'll give them to you. Bring them back here and feed the horses." Justin was unhappy. He dragged his feet, taking his own sweet time, muttering that his grandfather didn't love him any more, but he knew better than to argue, so he did as he was told.

It was the custom for the older people, both men and women, to make payday a social affair. The men would sit under the trees and talk or perhaps someone would start a game called 'three sticks.' When it finally became time to go home Justin helped hitch up the wagon again, and they started back to the canyon. In silence. Justin wouldn't even look at his grandfather. He was still hurting from losing those paints. When they got home, the boy unhitched the horses, then caught a goat that had to be held while her kid nursed. His chores done, he went inside, still ignoring the older man.

His grandfather called him. "Come sit over here by me, grandson." No, he didn't want to. But his grandfather called him again, and Justin was finally coaxed over. His grandfather reached into the pocket of his jacket and handed the boy the box of paints. "Here, grandson, go paint yourself a picture."

Justin did. A horse, of course. He worked and worked on it, and when it was finished he kept it between two pieces of cardboard, taking it out every day to admire it. The next trip to town, he took the picture with him. When a man at the store, who was himself an artist, asked if he would sell it, Justin nodded, and asked for five dollars.

That was the start of his career. His prices have gone up since then, but for a five year old in 1953, that was big money! He gave three dollars to his mother and spent the rest on a huge stick of candy that lasted him for days.

Justin's second school was a little farther off the reservation, in New Mexico where he entered the boarding school at Ft. Wingate. There again he ran into a lot of bullies who had lived a very easy life and would torment the ones who came from the reservation. At the beginning of his fourth grade year he decided he wanted to play basketball. They had a good team at the school, and by then his teachers were beginning to take more notice of him, probably, as he said, because he was just beginning to learn what school was all about. He started working really hard, and his efforts were appreciated. He stayed in that school for five years. One of the boys he met was Jim Abeita. They used to walk to the same art class together and became good friends. Justin considers him one of the finest of the Native American painters working today.

"When I was in the eighth grade I went to Oklahoma for three years, to the Fort Sill Indian School. Then I went back to the Chinle School. I studied hard, drew a lot of pictures, and I was the one who got the Art Award that year. After I graduated from High School I entered college at the University of California, studying electronics instead of art.

"It finally dawned on me that electronics was of no use on the reservation. I would have had to live in the city and that I didn't intend to do. I spent two and a half years at college, knowing it was the wrong place for me. In my third year I decided to volunteer for the Draft. I spent three years in the Army and got my honorable discharge in March, 1971.

"While I was still in the army I began to draw a lot of cartoons, and the military asked me to draw more so they could use them in a booklet about safety. I don't know what ever happened to all those drawings, and to the little booklet, but I would certainly like to find them.

"I had started drinking heavily and I realized I couldn't control it, but I couldn't stop, either. But when I woke up one day in a hospital, a young man of twenty-one, not knowing even how I had gotten there, I decided that was it. The doctor kept me in the hospital for a number of days, then sat me down for a long serious talk. He said, 'okay, son, you're going home. When you get there, I want you to give yourself at least a four or five day rest. Then Monday morning, I want you to go to this office,' and he gave me the address. I said okay.

"I didn't know that I was going to be a councilor for the AA program. I worked there over a year, and then the Tribe sent me up to the University of Utah, where they paid for my training in counseling, so I could learn how to deal with people and how to reach my fellow alcoholics. I worked for the AA program for five years.

"I knew then that it could be done. I had quit drinking, and alcohol could no longer control my life. But the best thing that happened to me in 1971 was meeting Evelyn, my wife. She has been a tremendous help to me ever since.

"Later, I started working for the Employment Agency, training young men - finishers, pipe layers, roofers - and I would send them out to different areas. The Tribe took action and helped them get employment. After that I went to work for the Veteran's Administration."

Justin left that job after several years when the case load got so big, telling the Administration to give others the jobs he knew they could handle. He went home and for about two weeks he just took it easy, staying with his wife and small family. Finally he decided to go up into the canyon and round up his horses. That was the start of his present way of living. In the Spring of 1979 he began leading groups of people who wanted to see the canyon in a more intimate way, from the back of a horse. He started with five horses. Evelyn was working for the Bureau of Indian Affairs, and Justin suggested she quit her job there. She was undecided, not wanting to leave a good paying position, but she finally asked for her release. Her supervisor told her the job would be waiting if she ever wanted to come back. It has been nineteen years now, and she never went back to the BIA. She is now an artist of a different caliber. She is a splendid cook, who keeps their guests happily filling their plates with authentic Navajo food on the trail rides.

In those years he went from three horses to fifty-two. His life revolves around his family, his horses and his art. He is widely traveled in this country, showing his unique paintings at many galleries such as the 4-Corner Gallery in Lambertville, New Jersey; the Heard Museum in Phoenix, Arizona; the Southwest Museum in Los Angeles, California; and at the Festival of Western Arts, where he has received many awards. His paintings hang in many private collections across the country.

"Sometimes people don't believe me, but when I was very small I was afraid of the dark. You know how kids are, afraid of unusual noises, so I used to sneak out and look around to see what it was I might be hearing. But after my mother passed on, it was different. My life was completely changed, and I am not afraid of the dark any more. I always say to her, 'Mother, take care of me.' And that's when I know that everything is really still, even in the dark. I like to feed my horses late, when it is dark, and I always know she is there, and my Grandpa is there. I used to get up early, before there was any sign of the dawn, to lead my race horses up into the canyon. I would suddenly feel a small breeze, and I would always say in Navajo, 'thank you, Grandpa.' I know that he is there."

The Navajo Way

The Navajos consider themselves the underground people who came up from the underworld through the four generations. Before that, there were insects and reptiles, birds and animals. The fourth world is the one the Navajo now inhabit. A Holy God contacted Mother Earth, and deep inside the womb of the earth, life was formed. As that life developed, it would come up through the first world, the second, the third and now the fourth. Through these journeys of immeasurable time, the clan system developed. Many things were seen as the people traveled: canyons, rivers, deserts. As they began to inhabit the earth, some might have seen a great body of water, and they would become the Edgewater Clan. Some might have passed an unusual dwelling and those became the Tower House Clan. Or perhaps a coyote crossed in front of someone, and he became a member of the Coyote Pass Clan.

The Clan system is very complicated, but there are rules that are respected. For instance, one may not marry within any of the four clans of the parents or grandparents. This prevents inbreeding and the stigma of incest.

Some think the Navajo are the Insect People, the title coming from the time they came up through the three worlds. There were many stories a young man had to learn in order to be called a wise man. When Navajo life was first laid down by the Holy One, he laid corn down on a buckskin, and the first man and first woman appeared before him. That's where the Holy People came from. The White Shell lady, and the White Shell Man, for instance. This is also where the early distaste for intermingling with other cultures began.

In the old Navajo way, when a young man was ready to get married, his family would look around for a young girl who would be a suitable bride. The girl was asked if she would take care of their son, cooking and keeping the hogan clean, taking care of the sheep or goats, grinding the corn, and doing all the things a wife should do. He, in turn, is asked by her parents if he will take care of their daughter, if he will haul water for his in-laws, take care of the horses, and do all the things a man should do to make a marriage, not only just between the bride and groom, but a marriage of the two family clans. If they both agree, a wedding date is set.

When Justin's father, Guy, was 17 and his mother, Alice, was 15, his grandfather, known as Navajo John, went over to the Tso's family and brought the young man back saying, *"you come home with me. I want you to support my daughter."* The young man went with his prospective father-in-law. That night he slept apart from the family, and the next morning, without saying anything to anyone, he went out to cut poles. He built his hogan in that one day.

Alice remembered that when they started living in the new

hogan, they didn't have even dishes. But soon members of both families started bringing them furnishings for their new home, pots or pans, a sheepskin or a rug.

In spite of Hollywood's habit of putting all Indians in tepees, the hogan was the traditional home of the Navajo people. It was round, and built of logs chinked with clay. There could be six or eight sides, and the entrance always faced east. When a man built a hogan, he was told to put a bear up over the door, either painted or carved. The bear's spirit would be his protection for the house and his family, keeping away bad or negative influences. If a man met a bear on a path away from the village, he was told to offer the bear sacred corn pollen and speak to it as though it were his grandfather, asking the bear to please go back to his own home and harm no one. The bear will listen and do no harm.

Sometimes, instead of a bear fetish, a hand made bow and arrow could be put over the door of the hogan, but there must be a real arrowhead on the head of the arrow.

In the old Navajo way, marriages followed a path set down centuries before. The families would get together and discuss what the bride was to be given, and how much the boy had to give to her family as a bride price, possibly a couple of ponies or a cow. The girl would be given instructions as how to best serve not only her husband, but his family. At the actual ceremony a medicine man is asked to officiate. He asks each in turn if he or she will take care of the other, and if they agree, it is the same answer....I do, or I will. The bride carries in the holy cornmeal in a basket,

and the boy carries the water in a two-handled wedding vase. The two go into the hogan and sit down with the medicine man. A little water is poured over their hands, and the girl is told to take some of the holy cornmeal and offer it to each of the four directions. The witnesses come in and each is given a taste of the cornmeal. The medicine man says they are now married.

Then in the Navajo way, the boy is warned not to cheat on his wife, to be faithful. But if he does cheat and she catches him at it, she may take his saddle and place it outside the hogan as a symbol that they are divorced. The girl is told the same thing, that the Holy People are watching, and if she cheats, there will be no place she can hide from their eyes that see everything. Then each member of the two families are given a chance to say whatever they would like to tell the new bride and groom. Finally, the couple is allowed to have the privacy of their new life together.

Children were loved and treated with great tenderness by the Navajo, not only the actual parents, but the grandparents, and aunts and uncles, who sometimes stood in for a parent. Children are not only the result of love between a man and his wife; they are the link between the traditions of the past and the hope of the future.

When a baby is born, when it first comes down to Mother Earth, the first thing it must do is cry, to show there is life. Then the mother is left alone for six months. She may not be bothered or touched during that time until she is completely healed. This gives her the precious time to bond with her baby, and for the baby to become used to its mother who is the source of nourishment and care. There is always an Indian name given the new child as well as the one he or she will use in the modern world. Justin's Indian name meant *"Man who ran around his enemy."* Two of the older great Navajo painters, friends of Justin, have equally meaningful names. Harrison Begay's is *"Warrior that approaches enemy"* and Beatin Yazz's name means *"Warrior that outran his enemy."*

Ceremonies were a very important part of Navajo life. Without them, how could a man know what his place was in the scheme of things? They were held for many reasons; probably the most important were the healing ceremonies.

There were many reasons a man might feel unwell. On the road he may have passed a place where a person of another culture had been; or perhaps an evil spirit. If there were bad spirits, it might cause a feeling of dizziness; or just feeling off balance; or his joints might swell. So songs were sung to the good spirits asking their protection against illnesses or distress. A young man was also taught what the dances and songs meant, and how they could affect a person.

Justin learned about the 'hand tremblers' who helped in time of stress. They would put corn pollen on their arm, then hold the hand outstretched and start talking to the Holy Ones. They would close their eyes and move their hands over the patient's body. By the movement of the air, or of the voices of the Holy Ones, which they alone could hear, the medicine men could envision what was wrong. They could tell what was affecting the physical system, or the mind, or the inner self. Then they would tell the sick person which ceremony he should have that would heal the sickness.

One day Justin felt sick and he went to a doctor. He was told there was nothing wrong, that he would feel better after a good night's sleep. In the morning when he still felt ill, his mother took him to a medicine man. He was told that the doctor had missed what was really wrong, that there were bad spirits hurting him, and a ceremony should be held.

"This particular time a friend went out to a sacred place to bring back some object, perhaps a shard of a pot made by the Anasazi, or a small object left there many years before. This object was tied up some way from my hogan. While the singing was going on I was disrobed and my body painted black with sheep fat mixed with charcoal. Then they trimmed me up with yucca leaves, so the sharp edges would keep the spirits away. One was put over my shoulder so the bad spirit would be gone permanently. Then a feather was tied that I had to keep with me. When all this was done, I was told to run fast over to where the little object was and shoot an arrow into it to destroy the bad spirit.

"But the next day, I still didn't feel good, so my mother took me to a hand trembler, and he said they had got it all wrong. They had brought back a piece of human bone which was not the correct thing to do. So the whole thing had to be done all over. But after that I felt well again."

"For generations , the horse has played a major part in the life of the Navajo. In their way of history, the Indian ponies were brought here by the Holy Ones. The men would sit in their hogans and say, 'you sit here and we'll light up the smoke and talk,' Then they would tell us the Holy Ones brought the white horse from the east. From the south , they brought the blue horse, the roan. The palominos, the yellow horses, came from the west. That's the reason so many Navajos carry the name yellow horse. This was the old belief, and if you believe it, okay; if you don't, okay.

"I think the Spaniards brought what we now call the mustang into this country. Many of them escaped when its rider might have been killed, and over many years, they bred and became the wild horses of the west. The Navajo horses of today are not really big, only about 14 hands. They are gentle, too. The most highly thought of horse, though, is the Appaloosa."

Justin tells a story about his grandfather, who was known as Navajo John, and his horses.The old man carried a medicine pouch that was to help him win races. When race time came, he would talk to the Holy People and ask them to help his horse win for him that day. His favorite was a little mare named Little Red. She was the fastest thing on four legs. Even some of the Hopi horses that were brought over to race against her couldn't beat her. He won so many races that the jealousy grew until one day the owners of some of the bigger horses got really angry and started whipping Justin's grandfather. Another family member stopped in and stopped the beatings. Some time later, he

got word from someone in Salt Lake City that there was going to be a race, and he wanted Navajo John to come there because they were really going to beat him. He only thought he had the fastest race horse! So Justin's grandfather said, "well, we'll see how good they are." He told the family he was going. So he got his saddle horse, his pack horse, a couple bags of grain, and Little Red.

They rode out through the mouth of the canyon and headed west. Camping along the way, it took him fifteen days to get from Chinle, Arizona to Salt Lake City, Utah.

He had made it a few days before the races, so he rested his horses, gave them grain and water. The next morning, Little Red was looking at him, as if she knew something important was about to happen. He got up and walked over to the little horse. "Okay," he said, "we've come a long way. You know how desperate we are. I've always taken the best care of you. Now I want you to win this race for me. How about it?" Justin said his grandfather told him that the little horse sniffed him all over, and that meant yes, the horse would win for him.

Race day came along, and Navajo John looked around for someone to jockey. He saw a young Mexican boy and asked him if he would ride Little Red. The boy agreed. "When he asked me how I wanted her handled, I told that boy just let her go." Time for the race to start, and the other horse owners started bringing their horses around. There was one really big horse, and his owner looked at Navajo John and said "I'm going to beat you." At least, that's what he thought the man said, since Mr. John had almost no English. But he replied in Navajo, hou, hou, meaning, okay, go ahead.

When the race started, that big horse came out ahead, and stayed ahead of the little mare, until they came to the turn. The Mexican boy merely flicked Red with his whip and she took off. She beat the field by three lengths. Everyone was yelling and hollering because most of them were betting on the big horse. Everyone wanted to know where that man and that little horse came from, and he told them he was from Navajo Land. He was so surprised because they paid him $25.00. That was a lot of money seventy years ago!

The next day he and his three horses started back to Chinle. They were still in Utah and he found a lovely place to camp, so he decided he would stay there a few days to rest up for the long trip back home. He tied his horses, built himself a nice little campfire, and was starting supper when he heard a long mournful howl. It got closer, then it was joined by several more. Wolves. They had smelled the horses. So Navajo John dragged up all the big logs and brush he could find, and kept a fire blazing all night. The horses were terrified, because there were so many wolves, but fortunately, their ropes held. The wolves came close enough to be seen in the moonlight, but the fear of the fire kept them at bay.

Justin's grandfather talked to the Holy Ones, asking them to take care of him and his horses. When daylight came, the wolves melted back into the forest. The man didn't stop even to eat breakfast; he just drew his gear together and doubletimed out of that area. It took them another thirteen days to get back to Chinle.

Hawk Shadow

What does the hawk see from the height
his great strong wings take him?
Do his eyes drink the beauty of the earth below?
Perhaps he sees only the timid mouse
crouching in fear in the tall grass.

Ceremonies

When a person felt ill, or thought he needed help in regaining his balance in life, a Ceremony would be held for him. Since the Navajo people are very family oriented, all the relatives and friends would gather to help with the healing.

The first night of the Ceremony the family would get together and decide where they would get a prayer stick. This had to be cut from a strong, straight juniper up on the mountains. The lower branches were trimmed off, leaving only a tuft of needles at the top. When it was brought back to the village, a bow and arrow was cut into the branch. These were symbols that would keep bad things away from the owner of the prayer stick. It was trimmed with eagle feathers, buckskin and sacred mountain dirt, turkey feathers and rabbit brush. The designs followed the way the Holy People had laid them out many, many years ago.

While the stick was being made and trimmed, relatives would gather, bringing different colored yarns for decoration, and there would be singing. The first night the sick person's relatives would say "we are going to bring you a prayer stick. How many days do you want us to sit before the Ceremony?" The sick person may say, "give me until Friday at 3:00 o'clock in the afternoon." Sheep and cash would be collected; the hand trembler would come, with people from other areas. There would be much singing and feasting. That first night of the Ceremony there was dancing, and the women had the right to choose their own partners, who in return were required to give the woman a bit of money. This is the squaw dance.

The medicine man would be singing to the Holy People, from the south, east, west and north, they who surround the land and the people. They each have different names, such as the white shell girl or the white shell boy, or the turquoise shell girl, or the corn pollen boy. The main one is called the Morning God, or the early morning person, to whom you could talk and ask for blessings. You might say, 'Before me I want good life; behind me I want good life; all around me I want good life.' That's the first thing you would ask that god..."*I ask you to grant me physical blessings - I want to be strong, I want to have good health, good muscles; my eyes to see good, my ears to hear good, my feelings to feel good. I want you to protect me so I can walk this life without any dangers.*"

The 'Good Way Ceremony' might be held if lightning struck near a person, hitting a rock or a tree. This could cause a great fright, which the person may dwell on too long. He may suddenly become afraid of rain, because there was a heavy rain at the time the lightning struck, so the two are mixed together in his mind. There would have to be a sand painting made for him, with streaks of lightning drawn with colored sand. Songs would be sung, helping put his mind back in balance so he wouldn't think too long on the bad effects of the lightning. Prayers and songs would be said and sung, asking for good rain, nice 'he' rain and soft 'she' rain. The 'he' rain comes down heavily and can cause lightning. Songs ask the Holy Ones to let the rain come down gently, and keep lightning away from the children. The 'she' rain is the kind that helps harvest the crops. It is a gentle, soaking rain that the earth can absorb. The 'she' rain is like a woman who raises you, bringing you up in a tender way, touching you gently.

The medicine men talk to the earth and to the sky, to the rocks and trees and the animals. They believe that everything has a spirit that can communicate with people. Justin's mother, when she was weaving, would talk to her rugs. She would say,

"we're going to finish here and we'll go to the market and you'll help me buy some good food." He used to listen to her, and thought what a wonderful way it was to shape things, even the wool.

I Remember My Horse

I remember my horse.
His delicate step.
I remember my horse.

I remember my horse,
His soft gleaming eye,
I remember my horse.

I remember my horse.
His proud arching neck.
I remember my horse.

I remember my horse,
His long flowing mane,
I remember my horse.

I remember my horse.
His dark satin coat,
I remember my horse.

I remember my horse,
The fire in his eye,
I remember my horse.

I remember my horse,
His smooth muscled back,
I remember my horse.

I dream of my horse,
The thundering hoofs,
I dream of my horse.

I dream of my horse.
My shield took the lance,
I dream of my horse.

I dream of my horse.
His heart took the thrust.
I dream of my horse.

I remember my horse.
I dream of my horse.
I remember my horse.

"The Warriors"

The well known Navajo artist, Beatin Yazz, had a great influence on the young Justin Tso. This picture, the Warriors, represents an idea Justin got from seeing a painting Yazz had done a number of years ago of two men fighting. It tells the story of two embattled groups who both wanted the same piece of land. So each sent a warrior out to fight to see which would win the land. The shields they carry are made of tough skin, goat or deer hide. One of the feathers represents each month. They are put on the shields for the warriors' protection. The lines in the air represent the disturbances from the fight, which could be either a death fight, or simply one to see which warrior will win the right to live on the disputed land. This painting was one of six that were featured in the magazine, "Art of the Southwest."

The Warriors

32" x 20"

"The Three Riders"

"I've always loved the earth colors, the purples in the distance views, and closer up, the orange and the red rocks. I paint many pictures with arches, to symbolize the land that surrounds us. But in the winter, when the spirits are asleep, the colors kind of fade out; and that's when the grey ones come in. But the land is always surrounding you....above you, before you. Those riders are going out to their relatives, to attend a Ceremony or a happening. When I was a child, we didn't have cars; horses were our mode of travel."

"The Three Riders" 20" x 16"

"Through The Valley"

"I don't know what you call those little yellow plants on the ground, but when you go out in that country you can see a lot of it, and the little white things above them represent the pollen. When I first started painting, I didn't put things like that in the pictures. But then I would go out and look at these yellow plants with the white puffy things on top, so I started putting them in, too.

"In this picture there is a little colt following along. Like all young animals, they like to be with their own family. I pretend in this painting that the people are going to a Yei-bei-chei Ceremony. They would be talking about the sand painting and how they will be sitting, and who will be helping to collect the colored sands so the painting will be correctly made for the healing ceremony."

Through The Valley

32" x 20"

"Shadow Riders"

The man on the horse is a medicine man . He is thinking about the horses that his grandfather or great, great grandfather used to ride. They are just memories now, spirits of the long ago horses. As the days come and go, he'll think maybe the past generations will visit him in his visions. When you look out there in the early evening you might see orange, turquoise blue, pinkish colors, and that's what these represent.

The man knows them well, but right now he is concentrating on trying to connect in spirit with those who have gone before.

This horse is a typical Indian pony, with the rather narrow neck and the almost Roman nose. This man is envisioning perhaps his own ancestors who rode their own ponies, like the one he now rides. In his imagination he sees them coming back, riding horses long dead, but always together in spirit. He is probably talking to them, just as though they were really there. Who is to say they are not?

"Sometimes I talk to my mother who has been gone several years now. I ask her, Mother, what are you doing now? I know it sounds crazy, but I feel her with me so often, and in my heart I know she still watches over me as she did when I was a small boy."

Shadow Riders

17″ x 8″

"A Strange Voice From the Sky"

Here are little horses, Navajo ponies. The Being in the sky used to own the mother and father of these ponies. He has passed on, but his spirit is there. He is talking to these horses through the airwaves, represented by the grey and white lines. His voice is coming through the Universe. The horses are alert, heads up, ears straight ahead, trying to find where the voice is coming from. He is telling the horses that his grandson will take care of them, giving food and clean water so they can have a good life, so they can run fast. The twelve feathers represent the years that they can reap the harvest of their friendship. The old man's grandson might race one of the horses, or just ride another and use one as a spare, but he will take good care of them. This is what the old man is telling them, and they listen.

"This old man had horses in the times when he was here....fat ponies and maybe horses that took a prize, or just riding horses. So when the young ones were born, he would say even horses have vision. My grandpa used to tell me that. When the horses were standing there, he would say 'the horses are talking to one another.' The man who owned the horses is sending messages down to the younger horses, to tell the little ponies to treat his grandson the right way.

"I wanted to put an Appaloosa in this painting. The Appaloosa is a very special breed to the Indian people. The man is talking to the horses, telling them to be good to his grandson, and always carry him here or there. The mane on the horse is the rein. You never cut it. His eyes would be the stars in the skies. You see, when a colt is born, he will fall out of his dam on the ground, and when he opens his eyes, he will always look at one star. That way, if you sell that horse and he goes a long way off with a new owner, he will always look at that star and find his way home. The curve of the neck is the rainbow, his tail is the rain. It, too, is never cut. You lift the foot up, and underneath is a frog, and you trim the hoof down and you will see an arrowhead. We believe the Holy People molded it. Where the Navajos have contact with that breed, the Appaloosa, it is a very special horse.

"You'll notice that every one of my paintings have some spiritual object...the people going to a Ceremony or a dance. And this one, when the people waiting for them see the horses coming, every medicine man and every man will start singing, and it's called the Horse Song. He'll mention the rainbow, and the rain, he'll mention the arrowhead, and the Holy Mountain. And maybe this man up here is singing the Horse song. That's why the horse is a very special animal, in the Navajo way.

"My grandpa had all these songs....songs that so many people have forgotten today. He had horse blessings, and even medicine bags for speed to win races. He might have dusted the speed off a humming bird, or one of those little striped lizards that are so fast. He would dust their speed into his medicine pouch. Then when the race time comes, he would talk to the Holy People and ask them to bless his horse, so he would win that day.

"My grandfather had race horses, six or seven, but three of them nobody could ever beat. He had a little mare, called Little Red, and even the bigger horses couldn't beat her. She raced in Hopiland, Flagstaff, Winslow...all around, places where the Navajos had match races. About a thousand yards from where my stables are, there is a rock that still sits there. That was the turn-around point during the races at Canyon de Chelly. I started out in the spring of 1983 with three horses. We now have fifty-two Indian horses. I started racing like my grandfather did, and at first my wife's older brother used to jockey. Today our son, Justin, Jr. is the jockey for our race horses."

A Strange Voice From the Sky   16" x 20"

"The Food Gatherers"

This painting represents the nine day healing Ceremony which takes place in the early part of the year, for a person who had been affected by early spring showers, or even snakebite. The men's bodies are painted white because they represent the healing gods, the Holy Ones. In order to conceal their own faces, they wear masks, made of buckskin, painted with blue colored sand. Their hair is made either from horse hair or black yarn.

The gods were put here on Mother Earth by the Holy People. They are from the four directions, and each has a name; from the East, the white shell woman, or the white shell boy; to the South, the turquoise woman, or the turquoise boy; to the west is the corn pollen woman, or the corn pollen boy; to the North is the black jade woman or the black jade boy.

The figure in the purple shirt in this painting is called the rainmaker. There again, he would have to do with the early spring thunder showers. The one centerleft, with the brown body, is the clown. He does things to make the kids laugh, and lighten up the ceremony when the crowd gets too serious. The figure down in front wearing the feathered headdress is the leader. He is the one who gives the corn pollen to the person being healed. The fox skins they are wearing are made for happy trails. The animals walk the earth and to them it is holy ground. The masked figures wear fine jewelry, turquoise necklaces and colorful skirts to honor the Holy Ones. The green ruffs around their necks are made of pine needles. On the fourth day of the Ceremony these men will go out to different houses and ask for food, or small change, which they carry in the small pouches made of the buckskin, and take back to distribute among the people.

There is a small hut built away from the sick person's hogan where these men will disrobe and paint their bodies white, then put on their gear. When they come out, they will have a small basket; in it is an eagle feather and some sacred corn pollen which they set down in front. The dancing and singing start, and when the Holy Ones hear the power of the singing, the feather in the basket will rise by itself and stand straight in the air. The people who are watching will know how powerful the Ceremony is, and are sure the sick person will be healed. When the singing and chanting is finished, the feather will return to the basket and those watching will know that this is truly a magical type of Ceremony.

There would be a large circle on the ground, brushed and smoothed. It is painted with colored sand, designed with figures of the yei gods. Pine needles, leaves, the different types of bushes, are all put in the sand painting. The sick person is brought out from his hogan and sits in the middle of the sand painting, while the singing and dancing lasts from early morning to the mid afternoon. When the ceremony is done and the healed person leaves, the sand is carefully gathered up on a cloth and disposed of in a sacred place where no one can touch it, no animal can get to it. It is left there, and gradually, it returns to the earth.

The Food Gatherers   22" x 17"

"Frightened By a Strange Voice From the Sky"

The deer in this painting are suddenly aware of something or someone above them. One of the sacred gods, the humpback Yei, is talking to them. He dances in the healing ceremony at night, so he carries the night and the stars, represented by the black area. The Yei has a rainbow around the shoulder area, and wears the red tailed hawk and the eagle feathers, which are considered sacred. The Navajo medicine men also use these same feathers to make fans, which are brushed over a person who has asked to be healed. The Yei carries a staff and a gourd which is rattled during the ceremony to chase all the bad things away from the ailing person . The bad spirits will disappear into the universe, and the person will be put back into balance and have a joyful and energetic life like these deer. They are painted blue, the sacred color for the south. Deer skin is used in many ways, for the dancers' pouches in the ceremony, and for their corn pollen bags. All parts of the deer are used, even the little hoofs are made into rattles.

Frightened By a Strange Voice From the Sky   16" x 22"

"The Singers"

These singers are at a ceremony. They have come, not only to take part, but to meet relatives and friends they may not have seen for months. Singing is a great part of Navajo life, so these singers represent the old traditions; they wear the traditional hats and colorful blankets, and are happily singing to the spirits that inhabit their world.

The Singers   16 ¹/₂" x 20"

"The Blue Rainbow"

The rainbow represents something good. After a rain, one can see the rainbow in the sky, and the Navajos would say, "there is a rainbow that will bring something good for you. Maybe good mental health, maybe good physical health or good financial help will come, all good things." The woman rides alone, heading for some relative's home, and she sees the bow in the sky, and she thinks of all the good things that are going to happen in her life. She might need a new robe or blanket; she might need new moccasins. She might be needing a new saddle for her horse, or a new bridle for her pony. When the Navajos wished for something, it was seldom a request for money; usually it was something they could use or wear; maybe she is thinking about a new bracelet.

The rainbow is colored blue, the sacred color of the south, and it is offering her something good. The wavy lines in the sky represent the movement of the air, or the clouds that form, change, and reform. The woman may close her eyes and hear in her mind the Holy Ones speaking to her through the air. She knows the rainbow always brings something good.

The Blue Rainbow   16″ x 20″

"The Fire Dancer"

When a person in the old days found himself off balance in his life, a Fire Dance Ceremony might be held for him. Similar to the Yei-bei-chei figures, this fire dancer's body is painted. He wears a mask, a short skirt, his moccasins, and carries juniper bark in his hand. When the big fire is built, he ignites the bark and then dances around the fire, then hurls the lighted bark into the air away from the crowd. It will fly a long way, and light up the surrounding area like fireworks on the Fourth of July. This is a part of a healing ceremony that may last four nights or possibly even eight.

The Fire Dancer   11" x 17"

"Food Gatherers III"

This painting is another representation of a healing ceremony.
The figure on the left is the humpback Yei, one of the main
healers. He carries the night, the staff and gourd. The four
sacred colors from Mother Earth, black, white, blue and yellow,
are part of his dress. The figure on the right is called the
Morning God. He carries on his back the sacred sage. He is
holding the skin of a young kit fox, which he swings out and
drives away all illness from the sick person. The central figures
represent the Yei gods, who perform their part of the healing
ceremony. They also wear kit fox hides.

Food Gatherers III   22" x 17"

"Young Friends"

This young colt wandered off away from his mother and comes across this new friend, the blue fawn. They start to play, and it grows dark. They are still happy with their newfound friendship. Finally a crescent moon comes out and a little bird joins them. It is a picture that recalls the innocent happiness of the very young. Again, Justin has used the sacred color blue to illustrate this charming scene and the joy that comes when the young heart is uncluttered with troubles.

Young Friends   11" x 14"

"Headin' For Lower Country"

These people are going back into the valley as winter approaches. They have spent the cool summer months in the mountains, and now it is time to go lower where the sun will warm them and where the snows are not so deep. They are riding through the aspens, which grow in the mountains, and they cross the water on their way to warmer quarters. When they get back to their hogans, they will prepare for the coming winter, bringing in wood and a water supply. Behind them, not shown in the picture, is their wagon, loaded with the food they have grown in the summer, which will provide for them during the cold months. Their sheep are following, since they could not survive the deep snows in the high country.

Headin' For Lower Country   14" x 12"

"Riding With the Humpback"

The Navajos are heading for a Yei-bei-chei ceremony. There are young people with them going along to be taught as they watch the older people during the dances and the singing. Then when they are older, they will know how to take part in the Ceremony.

The girl may become one of the women who perform the Squaw Dance. The young man may take the part of one of the Yei gods.

The humpback Yei watches over them during their journey, making sure that they do not meet trouble on the way, that they arrive safely. He is always a part of the Ceremony, and a blessed figure in Navajo life.

Riding With the Humpback

20″ x 16″

"The Food Gatherers II"

This painting illustrates in detail the masks worn by those representing the holy Yei gods. The one on the upper left is the clown mask. Just below that is the mask worn by the head of the group. The black one belongs to the rainmaker. The blue mask is worn by the one representing the humpback Yei. The yellow ruffs under the masks are made of buckskin, painted and beaded.

The Food Gatherers II

20" x 26"

"Yei-bei-chei Dancers"

This painting represents the second night of the Yei-bei-chei dance, in which the women take part. They are carrying pine brushes and are dressed traditionally. The background shows an area some thirty miles from Justin's home in Chinle, a place called Round Rock. It is late evening, and the light from the west is just catching the mountain in the background, as the sun is low in the sky. The colorful costumes, the graceful movement of the women dancers, and the authority of the Yei figures is stunning.

Yei-bei-chei Dancers

34″ x 24″

"Fire Dancers"

Late at night, when the moon is high, the participants dance around the huge bonfire. They carry brushes made of the sacred juniper, which they light from the fire, and after dancing and singing, they toss the lighted brushes high in the air, driving away evil spirits, and bringing balance to the people being healed. Sometimes the fire is thrown into the crowd, but no one is ever burned. The background again shows Justin's love for his own part of the world, the rocks, the terrain with the almost ghostly formations, and above all, the mystery of the night when the Holy Ones walk among his people.

Fire Dancers

34" x 23"

"Packin' It In"

"In the days of my grandfolk's time, we hunted only once a year. This way the tribe was furnished with meat, but we didn't slaughter the animals needlessly. We took only what was necessary for the coming winter. We would go either on foot, or on horseback, and when we came to a place where a deer had been seen, we would set up camp. We would always try to be sure it was a safe place for us and for our horses."

The gear would be unpacked, a sheepskin and blankets for chilly nights, and the hunter would stay in camp until he got his game. When the deer was killed, it was skinned immediately where it was shot. Only the meat would be taken. The bones and innards were buried on the spot, in the sacred and correct way according to custom. The man in the picture has already killed his deer and is packing it home.

Packin' It In

"The Wedding"

The bride and groom sit in their new hogan with the Medicine man. He is giving them the instructions all young couple must receive, and they are seriously listening to his words. The bowl of corn pollen, the wedding vase, the dress of the bride, are all symbols of the Ceremony.

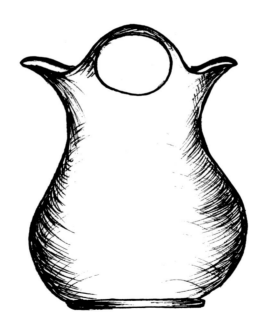

The Wedding   22″ x 18″

"The Long Walk"

The Long Walk began in 1864. Some of the young Navajo men had begun stealing into the army forts and taking food and guns. When they were discovered, the battles between Indian and army resulted in General Carlton sending Kit Carson to round them up and move them to Ft. Sumner, New Mexico. The Navajos discovered that Carson, whom they called Red Hair, was coming after them, so thinking that only the women and children would be taken, the young men went to the mountains and cut four long poles from Ponderosa trees and dragged them all the way back to Canyon de Chelly. There is a place called the Navajo Fortress Rock, and this is where they put the poles and used them to climb up to safety.

While they were there, the army couldn't reach them; but unfortunately, in time the food and water ran out; many of the people there took sick and some died. The Navajos had to come down and surrender. Kit Carson started them on the long walk. They went first to what is now Ft. Defiance, and from there, about eight thousand Navajos were forced to walk nearly five hundred miles to New Mexico. The canyon where they held out for so long is known as Canyon del Muerto, the canyon of death. Many of the people died on that long walk and they were buried along the way. Those who tried to escape were shot. Some of the young girls were taken by the soldiers and raped, or sold as slaves to other tribes.

When they got to New Mexico they found the land was not fit for farming. The crops the Navajos tried to raise didn't survive, and food became scarce. They begged the Army to send them home, but it took four long bitter years before a chief named Barbecito managed to convince the government to let the people go. A hand written treaty was drawn up, signed with the thumb prints or marks of several Navajo leaders. It was given to General Carlton, and finally the long walk began again, this time back to the Canyon.

Many died on the way, but those who finally made it home were met by the few who had escaped when the soldiers came, and welcomed them back. Justin's great, great, grandparents were on that long walk. His grandfather's mother was a child of eight when they started , and her uncle carried her part of the way on his back. She was one of the children who managed to hide from the soldiers who were trying to take the girls and sell them. This remarkable woman died in 1958 at the age of 103 years.

Canyon de Chelly was the homeland of these people. The great chief, Barbecito, who helped them get home, is buried somewhere in the canyon, but like Moses, his grave is hidden and no one knows just where.

When the people came back, some began to move out of the Canyon toward Utah, or along the San Juan river. They replanted their peach trees that had been destroyed and grew pumpkins, squash, corn and watermelons. They held their sacred ceremonies that helped bring them back into balance with Mother Earth and Father Sky. But never will they forget what they had to endure.

The Long Walk   26" x 21"

In Memoriam

I would go home and lay me down beneath a pinon tree.
Ah-hai, the hogans are deserted now.

My soul is heavy, and my throat thick with unshed tears.
Ah-hai, the hogans are deserted now.

My people eat despair, and drink the bitter water of bondage.
The little ones draw hopelessness from their mothers' breasts.
The young men turn their faces to the ground and stand no
longer erect.
Ah-hai, the hogans are deserted now.

The desert Gods who ride the wind grow restless of their waiting.
Who will gather the sacred pollen? Who will chant the sunrise
song? Who will dance for the Holy Ones?
Ah-hai, the hogans are deserted now.

I would go home and lay me down to die.
No one will slay my horse. No one will turn my face to the east.
No one will tie my feet. My soul will wander forever.

But I would go home to die.
Ah-hai, ah-hai, the hogans are deserted now.

The Present

"The Navajo Tribe has come to me several times and asked me to work with the young people, to tell them about my paintings, why they represent an earlier way of life, and what the symbols I put into them mean. This was a way of life that is being forgotten. I tell them I grew up on the edge of that old way, and how horses were so much a part of our lives, how I grew up in the canyon, how we used to travel with wagons instead of cars. They asked if there was a lot of alcohol or drugs in those days. I tell them, no, we had a whip in the corner and if we had to be told to do something twice, the second time was emphasized with that whip! Sometime Eddie, my nephew, will go out with the kids and talk to them. He tells them about our horses, our programs, what we offer. We take the kids on trail rides, three days and nights. This is paid for by the Tribe. My son, Justin, Jr, takes them out sometimes, teaching them riding, how to take care of the horses and learning who they really are, what their background means, and why they should take pride in being Navajo.

"Our number one problem right now is alcohol and drugs. If that problem is not met and controlled, the next step can lead to real disaster. We try to keep the kids busy with the horses, learning about the canyon country, teaching them what dangers lie ahead if they get in with the wrong crowd. It is a good program.

"In 1974 I started working with the Veteran's Administration. Many of the Navajos had been in both WWII and Korea, and had seen a part of the world and a life they had never known. So many of them, when they got out of the service, didn't know they had benefits coming to them. I saw veterans who had been wounded in action, but they never got benefits or compensation from the Government. I went up to Window Rock and tried to find out what was going on.

"I spent a great deal of my own money and time on the telephone calling St. Louis, Missouri, asking about the veterans who were not receiving any help. There was a lot of paper work involved. Many of the discharge papers had the initials WWA on them, meaning wounded while in action. So many men had no idea that they should have been receiving compensation because they had been wounded. After they were discharged, they had six months in which they could receive compensation if they were hurt while on a job, but again, they didn't know it.

"There were about six of us working with the Administration. My office was in Chinle, but there were offices in Shiprock, Tuba City, Keyenta and Crown Point. We had a huge case load, but we worked hard at it and got a lot of back pay for the veterans. The now famous Code Talkers were not recognized for many years. I believe that at present there are only a few still living. We are all proud that the Government has recently awarded those few the Medal of Honor.

"I worked for the Administration for five years, which I felt was long enough. I wanted to get back to my roots, to the canyon where I was born."

Squash Blossom

Gleaming gold, lying softly on the tender brown earth,

Holding within its open blossom the future fruit,

The squash blossom flaunts its beauty for any to see.

Richly formed, attracting the hungry bee,

Giving its pollen unstintingly to the first passerby,

Squash blossom, lasting only a few days.

A gift to man from the Holy Ones, and the promise

Of renewing life.

Shining silver, lying proudly on warm brown skin,

Silently singing the artist's excellence;

The squash blossom displays its symmetry to an admiring world.

Delicately, strongly formed, attracting envious glances,

Swinging with every turn of a Navajo's dancing body,

Squash blossom. An eternal symbol

Of the artist's praise to his God.

Art in its many forms has become a way of life for the Navajo people, as well as for the other tribes. And the work of each different tribe is easily recognized. The silver Indian jewelry as we know it is comparatively new. We forget that ancient burials have shown that jewelry was used centuries and centuries ago. People were buried with shell necklaces, horn or antler artifacts, and bits of stones such as jade and turquoise. Coral was obtained by trading with the peoples living along the coast lines and was highly sought after.

Today the Native American artist works not only in silver, which was for many years the material of choice, but in gold and other metals as well, and has begun using many stones other than the familiar turquoise. There are many jewelry pieces today that emphasize lapis lazuli, opal, tourmaline, onyx, carnelian and even diamonds.

Weaving is truly a fine art. The Navajo women tend their sheep, some shear the wool, card and spin it, and spend hours at the loom weaving a pattern that they do not usually have on paper. It is in the mind of the weaver. Some of the rugs or blankets seen today are worthy of any good museum, and should and do command extremely high prices.

Basketry, particularly the really old baskets, bring astronomical prices. It takes many hours to gather the grasses, sort and dry them, and then weave the hundreds of fine blades into the patterned baskets that range from the minute to the great ones that were used for storage.

Those of us who collect the lovely pots, recognize and appreciate the work that goes into them. Finding just the right clay, adding the frit, making the coils, paddling the pot to mold it, then smoothing the clay with a stone that may have been handed down from grandmother to mother to daughter; aware that all of this work might possibly be destroyed if in the firing the pot cracks - these long hours never bring nearly enough money to the maker for the time spent.

There are many fine Native American artists working today in different mediums. Paintings, sculptures, alabaster and marble, bronze, and of course, the traditional silver and turquoise, which more than any other medium, is representative of the American Indian. Bolas, concha belts, necklaces of all kinds, bracelets, rings and earrings, belt buckles, all are proudly displayed at 'powwows' and Indian fairs, as well as shops across the country.

The most important part of all this beautiful work is the underlying meaning. The artist, painter or silversmith, works not only for the creation of the piece. A woman who is making a pot is thinking of the spirit of the pot. Perhaps it will bring her money, which she needs to buy something. She may be making it for herself, and as she coils the clay, she might be singing a blessing to the little pot, asking that it will not crack in firing, and that it will be strong and hold the food that will feed her family.

When Justin paints a picture he thinks of more than design

and color. His paintings tell a story, his way of bringing back some of the traditions and beliefs of his people, stories that may be forgotten if someone does not leave a record of them.

He came from a family of artists and weavers, and he has passed his talents on to the next generation. His son, Justin, Jr., is fast becoming a fine painter. A nephew, Eddie, who works with him leading rides through the canyon, can handle a pencil or a paint brush well. The spirit of Justin's grandfather, and the spirit of his mother are always with him and the little pine tree that began its life when he did, is still there, growing strong on the slope of the canyon wall.

Justin Tso. Navajo. Artist. Raconteur. A man with his feet planted firmly in two cultures. Living simply, but keeping the mantle of dignity about him. Knowing his own worth as a man and as an artist, but never losing the humility that all truly great artists must have. Living in a world that has not always been kind to his people, but accepting it without bitterness. A man generous to a fault, raising not only his own family, but nephews and grandchildren as well. A complex individual, acknowledging the modern world, while teaching the traditions and beliefs of his forefathers. Putting into his paintings the sacred symbols of the Diné so those who come after him may look and remember.